SURE SUCCESS IN ENGLISH GRAMMER, TENSES, ASPECTS,
ARTICLES AND LETTERWRITING
Copywright © Onye kingsley 2014

All Rights Reserved

No part of this book may be reproduced in any form by photocopying or by any electronic or mechanical means, including information storage or retrieval systems, without permission in writing from both the copyright owner and the publisher of this book.

ISBN 978-0-9569415-8-9

First Published 2014 by
KINGSLEY PUBLISHERS (UK) LTD.
76 Foxcombe Fieldway Addington Village
Cr0 9ez,
Croydon
London.
www.kingsleybooks.co.uk

Printed for KINGSLEY PUBLISHERS.

"SURE SUCCESS" OBJECTIVE MODEL Q & A's IN ENGLISH LANGUAGE EXAMS

OBJECTIVE TEST

In each of the following sentences, there is one word or group of words underlined and one gap. From the list of word lettered A to E, choose the word or group of words that is <u>most nearly opposite in meaning to the underlined word</u> and that will, at the same time, correctly fill the gap in the sentence.

1. The <u>dissident</u> soldiers were crushed by the………troops.

    A. rebellious

    B. courageous

    C. brave

    D. honest

    E. loyal

2. Aliyu's <u>humility</u> contrasts with the ….of his eldest brother

    A. beauty

    B. haughtiness

    C. ugliness

    D. achievement

    E. prominence

3. The ring I am wearing is…while Bola's is an <u>imitation</u>

    A. silvery

    B. fake

C. perfect

D. genuine

E. golden

4. Shallow minds would not be able to appreciate the ...arguments of the professor.

   A. profound
   B. special
   C. excellent
   D. bombastic
   E. established

5. Nwafor is always taciturn while Chike is usually very...

   A. officious
   B. ridiculous
   C. ambitious
   D. dexterous
   E. loquacious

6. Thomas was...about the enterprise but Peter was convince that it would succeed.

   A. critical
   B. confident
   C. sceptical
   D. reluctant
   E. different

7. The lawyers wanted the newly promulgated decree to be...

   A. repealed

   B. condemned

   C. disproved

   D. revised

   E. expunged

From the words lettered A to E, choose the word or group of words that best completes each of the following sentences

8. The Supreme Court...the Judgement of the lower court.

   A. abused

   B. nullified

   C. attacked

   D. proclaimed

   E. invited

9. The...of the late minister will be laid to rest tomorrow

   A. fossils

   B. ashes

   C. remains

   D. skeleton

   E. burial

10. The prostitute is facing a charge of…following the suspicious death of her new baby.

    A. abortion

    B. regicide

    C. fratricide

    D. manslaughter

    E. infanticide

11. The guest spoke just for a minute and many of the people present admired him for his…

    A. obscurity

    B. clarity

    C. verbosity

    D. brevity

    E. intellect

12. The secret act was…to me by his secretary

    A. breathed

    B. revealed

    C. screened

    D. whispered

    E. published

13. Opara speaks one of the many…of Igbo language.

    A. dialects

    B. utterances

    C. phonetic

    D. sounds

E. assents

14. The teacher advised Akpan to make his handwriting more....

   A. sonorous
   B. tangible
   C. remarkable
   D. legible
   E. credible

After each of the following sentences, a list of possible interpretations of the sentence is given. Choose the interpretation that you consider appropriate for each sentence.

15. No matter what people may say, I expect Wahab to stand his ground. This means that Wahab should

   A. stand on hard grounds
   B. refuse to listen to others
   C. remain erect rather than fall
   D. maintain his position.

16. The rebel did not pull his punches in his attack against the ruler. This means that the rebel

   A. was eventually captured by men loyal to the ruler
   B. condemned the ruler very vigorously
   C. failed in his attempt to escape arrest.
   D. Threw some punches when he was about to be arrested.

17. Femi developed cold feet when he was asked to lead the protest march. This mean that Femi was

    A. afraid

    B. sick

    C. courageous

    D. doubtful

18. The man and his wife have been living a cat-and-dog life. This means that they

    A. have always been quarreling

    B. find it difficult to make ends meet

    C. keep cats and dogs as pets

    D. are living like neighbours

19. Living with Kunle is a tax on one's patience. This means that

    A. Kunle is a pleasant person to live with

    B. Staying with Kunle requires extreme endurance

    C. Kunle does not pay his tax as and when due

    D. Kunle is always very patient.

20. Ibrahim took his friend's advice with a pinch of salt. This means that Ibrahim

    A. valued the advice

    B. regretted taking the advice

    C. was sceptical about the advice

    D. felt the advise was insulting

21. Nobody thought the two friends would cross swords with each other over that matter. This means that the friends

    A. had a serious disagreement

    B. exchanged gifts of swords

    C. re-affirmed their love for each other

    D. were advised to settle the matter peacefully.

From the words lettered A to E below each of the following sentence, choose the word that is nearest in meaning to the underlined word as it is used in the sentence.

22. The cattle egret is one of the migratory birds in this part of the world.

    A. seasonal

    B. aerial

    C. permanent

    D. typical

    E. temporary

23. His strident voice reverberated all through the hall.

    A. lyrical

    B. coarse

    C. musical

    D. soft

    E. shrill

24. Yahaya is very lackadaisical in his approach to his studies

    A. unenthusiastic

    B. involved

    C. unsatisfactory

    D. repulsive

    E. rebellious

25. There was pandemonium in the town as soon as his name was announced as the next ruler.

    A. jubilation

    B. disorder

    C. enjoyment

    D. dancing

    E. danger

26. The loan facility is only for indigent students

    A. privileged

    B. clever

    C. poor

    D. brilliant

    E. rich

27. The people called on the new ruler to relinquish the title

    A. maintain

    B. cherish

    C. protect

    D. renounce

    E. release

From the words or group of words lettered A to D, choose the word or group of words that best completes each of the following sentences.

28. Our aeroplane landed…Kano Airport.

    A. by

    B. on

    C. in

    D. at

29. Ade was late…..school this morning.

    A. in

    B. for

    C. to

    D. at

30. Every culture has unique customs associated………eating

    A. with

    B. to

    C. over

    D. about

31. The housemaster called the troublemaker .....the office for a warning.

    A. inside

    B. into

    C. at

    D. in

32. What .....these last two years?

    A. have you being doing

    B. had you been doing

    C. you have been doing

    D. have you been doing

33. While the old man.....by thugs, other ruffians set his house on fire.

    A. was been assaulted

    B. would have been assaulted

    C. has been assaulted

    D. was being assaulted

34. Our school dance didn't succeed as we had hoped........?

    A. hadn't it

    B. has it

    C. isn't it

    D. did it

35. You actually saw him go through the window…..?

    A. is t

    B. didn't you

    C. didn't he

    D. did he

36. Nkechi went to Port Harcourt yesterday,…….?

    A. did she to

    B. isn't it

    C. didn't she

    D. wasn't it.

37. There were not students on the campus yesterday………?

    A. weren't there

    B. were they

    C. were there

    D. weren't they

38. I'm afraid I couldn't lend you my dictionary; I …..it then.

    A. am consulting

    B. will be consulting

    C. would be consulting

    D. was consulting

39. By the end of this year, i………….here for 20 years.

    A. will have been working

    B. have been working

    C. would be working

    D. shall be working

40. If there ……no change in the wealth, we would have started yesterday.

    A. had been

    B. had being

    C. would be

    D. is

41. A decent girl…….take notice of street boys who make rude comments.

    A. doesn't need

    B. shouldn't

    C. don't need to

    D. couldn't

42. That brother of…………….is always in financial difficulty.

    A. hers'

    B. hers

    C. her's

    D. her.

43. I'm sure the new boy,........,will join our house team.

    A.   that is he is related to several well-known athletes.

    B.   He is related to several well-known athletes

    C.   Was related to several well-known athletes

    D.   Who is related to several well-known athletes

44. Learning how to drive a car is.......difficult than learning how to ride a bicycle.

    A.   either more

    B.   any more

    C.   no more

    D.   neither more

45. Chike had trouble digging up the yam tuber because the soil..........very hard.

    A.   is

    B.   was being

    C.   was

    D.   has been

46. You ....as I don't require the car immediately.

    A.   needn't rushing

    B.   needn't to rush

    C.   need not to rush

    D.   needn't have a rush

47. It's a shame that she encountered such discourtesy ………?

    A. can't she

    B. didn't she

    C. didn't it

    D. isn't it

48. The beggar who is feeling his way down the road…….be blind

    A. should

    B. would

    C. must

    D. ought to

49. Mrs. Ojo instructed her daughters…….past the Heavenly Beer Bar.

    A. not to have walked

    B. that they would not walk

    C. not to walk

    D. against not to walk.

50. I am looking forward……my parents again.

    A. in seeing

    B. to seeing

    C. to see

    D. to seen

51. I know I want one of these blouses, but I can't decide............

    A. which one

    B. that one

    C. there one

    D. what one

52. She needs......new clothes before she begins her office

    A. a few

    B. little

    C. a little

    D. few.

53 Why did you resign from your former post....this one in Kaduna

    A. into

    B. to

    C. towards

    D. for

54. During the harmattan, large months are attracted to the lights.......

    A. in night

    B. during night

    C. at night

    D. by night

55. If he……..of her past behaviour, John would not have married Mary.

    A. has known

    B. had known

    C. have known

    D. was known

56. I'm….pleased with this dress now than when I bought it.

    A. quite

    B. even

    C. fairly

    D. more

57. Members of the expedition became desperate when their supplies……..

    A. ran out

    B. ran off

    C. finished off

    D. faded away.

58. …….what you said last week, Aret, I disagree with your proposal for higher fees

    A. on the side of

    B. relating back to

    C. with reference to

    D. withdrawing from

59   I hope your sister is no…….suffering from malaria.

   A.   longer

   B.   more

   C.   further

   D.   farther

60. My sister arrived in Port Harcourt from Kaduna yesterday so she…….to the humidity yet.

   A.   hadn't adjusted

   B.   hasn't adjusted

   C.   didn't adjusted

   D.   haven't adjusted

61. There would have been a breakdown of law and order two days ago if the officials………..the riot.

   A.   do not quell

   B.   have not quelling

   C.   were not quelling

   D.   had not quelled.

62. Mrs. Bassey later served a delicious meal, ……..she had burnt the stew.

   A.   despite

   B.   ever since

   C.   since

   D.   even though

63. ……..our request, the school choir sang another spiritual hymn.

    A.   at

    B.   by

    C.   unto

    D.   with

64. ………..have a right to government assistance

    A.   The blinds

    B.   A blind

    C.   The blind

    D.   Blinds

65. Could you please ………a receipt for my purchase?

    A.   make up

    B.   make out

    C.   make for

    D.   make over

In the following passage the numbered gaps indicate missing words. Against each number in the list below the passage. Five choices are offered in columns lettered A to E. For each question, choose the word that is the most suitable to fill the numbered gap in the passage.

PASSAGE

Olu is the best photographer in town, very adept in the use of -66-. His -67- is fully air-conditioned so that the many -68- who come to him for -69- can relax and feel comfortable in the well-furnished waiting room. Quickly, he would feed the -70- into his expensive 35mm camera from Japan, focus the -71- and, before you know what is happening, press the shutter release -72-. He has taken the photograph.

Soon, he hurries into the -73- and takes out the film to be -74- into a -75-. A few minutes later, he strides out, examine the result against the light, and nodding his head in satisfaction goes back to -76- it into a beautiful -77-.

I do not know any professional with so much -78-. His camera has many -79- which he fits into one side or the other and has an enlarger with which he increases the -80- of a picture for printing.

	A	B	C	D	E
66.	film	projector	camera	microscope	telescope
67.	sitting room	factory	laboratory	workshop	studio
68.	patients	customers	consultants	attendants	patrons
69	consultation	snapshots	exposure	passports	advice
70.	tape	battery	chemicals	cassette	film
71.	lens	shutter	aperture	timer	video
72.	flash	winder	lens	knob	gun
73.	store	strong room	dark-room	theatre	clinic
74.	enlarged	manufactured	printed	exposed	developed
75.	negative	shadow	substance	profile	positive
76.	embellish	print	define	refine	stamp
77.	craft	artefact	image	work	picture
78.	equipment	property	furniture	item	material
79.	instruments	attachments	accessories	conveniences	models
80.	quantity	quality	brightness	size	length

From the words lettered A to D, choose the word that has a similar word with the unlined sound in the given word.

81. hate

   A. honour
   B. heir
   C. hut
   D. hour

86. follow

   A. fellow
   B. fold
   C. hot
   D. pork

82. c<u>ou</u>ld
   A. c<u>o</u>ld
   B. p<u>u</u>t
   C. t<u>ou</u>gh
   D. m<u>ou</u>ld

83. <u>th</u>igh
   A. <u>d</u>ye
   B. <u>th</u>en
   C. <u>t</u>ie
   D. <u>th</u>ink

84. <u>p</u>resident
   A. <u>p</u>recedent
   B. <u>p</u>ress
   C. <u>p</u>osh
   D. <u>p</u>rize

85. <u>p</u>ea<u>c</u>e
   A. <u>g</u>ree<u>d</u>
   B. <u>p</u>i<u>ss</u>
   C. <u>p</u>a<u>c</u>e
   D. <u>g</u>ri<u>d</u>

87. ki<u>ng</u>
   A. ki<u>ck</u>
   B. ha<u>ng</u>er
   C. hi<u>ng</u>e
   D. <u>n</u>eighbour

88. fa<u>c</u>e
   A. va<u>s</u>e
   B. ba<u>s</u>e
   C. pha<u>s</u>e
   D. pa<u>c</u>e

89. <u>a</u>bout
   A. <u>a</u>rt
   B. b<u>a</u>g
   C. l<u>a</u>ter
   D. <u>a</u>gain

90. <u>air</u>
   A. <u>ear</u>
   B. <u>heir</u>
   C. <u>here</u>
   D. <u>ire</u>

From the words lettered A to D, choose the word that rhymes with the given word.

91. leader

    A. hunter

    B. reader

    C. other

    D. matter

92. half

    A. have

    B. curve

    C. cuff

    D. laugh

93. deceit

    A. receipt

    B. polite

    C. recite

    D. resit

94. know

    A. how

    B. knot

    C. no

    D. nought

95. port

    A.   shirt

    B.   shut

    C.   short

    D.   shot

In each of the following questions, the main/primary stress is indicated by writing the stressed syllable in capital letters. From the words lettered A to D, choose the one that has the correct stress.

96. indignation

    A.   indigNation

    B.   INdignation

    C.   IndignaTION

    D.   InDIGnation

97. education

    A.   educaTION

    B.   eDUcation

    C.   eduCATion

    D.   Education

98. political

    A.   POlitical

    B.   poLItical

    C.   poliTIcal

    D.   politiCAL

99. mathematics

    A. maTHEmatics

    B. MAthematics

    C. mathemaTICS

    D. matheMAtics

100. development

    A. DEvelopment

    B. developMENT

    C. deveLOPment

    D. deVElopment

In the following passages the numbered gaps indicate missing words. Against each number in the list below each for each question, choose the word that is the most suitable to fill the numbered gap in the passage.

PASSAGE A

When anyone hears his own voice played back to him one a –101-, he is usually shocked and baffled. Something must be allowed for the –102- of the –103- -104-, but it is quite common for –105- to find that his –106- is not shared by his friends. The conclusion must be that we do not always know how our own –107- -108- to other people, and our ignorance applies both to general impression and to details of –109-. Probably most of us found that there are days when everybody seems to be –110- and other days when everybody seem to be –111-. The most likely explanation is that people are –112- to our own –113- as expressed in our –114-, which seems to us to be perfectly –115-.

	A	B	C	D	E
101.	radio	tape	amplifier	cartridge	phone
102.	falsehood	sins	offence	imperfections	accuracy
103.	printing	practical	physiological	chemical	mechanical
104.	recording	reporting	diluting	waxing	taping
105	writer	singer	speaker	recorder	taper
106.	gullibility	incredibility	animosity	objectivity	profanity
107.	music	hiccup	noise	grumbling	voice
108.	muffles	chants	echoes	sounds	grunts
109.	communications	pronunciation	annunciation	declaration	words
110.	hostile	suspicious	friendly	homely	gay
111.	irritable	truthful	invincible	honest	fastidious
112.	corresponding	responding	alternating	retaliating	opposing
113.	opinion	affairs	status	position	mood
114.	song	lyrics	intonation	rhyme	poem
115.	pleasant	unusual	abnormal	normal	abstract

PASSAGE B

The –116- of the natural resources of the –117- constitutes the –118- system of any –119-, and the –120- of this system in 121- time. The first point, which must be mentioned, is the –122- of work. As we have said, most –123- effort in primitive –124- is devoted to the production of food. The –125- involved in this have, quite part form the –126- of real or –127- hunger, led to a –128- interest lacking in the ordinary work of an office or factory in contemporary civilization. This will become clear when we reflect that most of the –129- activities of primitive peoples, such as fishing, hunting and gardening, are –130- among us.

	A	B	C	D	E
116.	exploration	exploitation	mining	harvesting	enjoyment
117.	ground	locality	town	area	environment
118.	productive	providing	work	cultural	agrarian
119.	person	people	cottage	cultural	family
120.	running	style	manner	organization	organ
121.	primeval	ancient	primitive	primary	original
122.	type	character	way	method	system
123.	economic	financial	monetary	fiscal	gainful
124.	times	societies	peoples	men	citizens
125.	actions	reactions	activities	measures	means
126.	stimulant	stimulus	fear	danger	feeling
127.	paralyzed	imagined	imminent	reared	probable

128. keen   spontaneous   real   big   vested

129. meaningful rewarding   gainful   scrounging   important

130. unnecessary useless   recreational meaningless   valueless

In each of the following sentences, there is one word underlined and one gap. From the list of words or group of words lettered A to E, choose the word or group of words that is most nearly opposite in meaning to the underlined word and that will, at the same time, correctly fill the gap in the sentence.

131. The author wrote more <u>comedies</u> than……..

    A.   plays

    B.   novels

    C.   tragedies

    D.   poems

    E.   scenes

132. Mary is a <u>frugal</u> house wife but her husband is……..

    A.   rich

    B.   extravagant

    C.   poor

    D.   free

    E.   economical

133. A _comprehensive_ report of the incident is necessary because anything ......will be inadequate.

    A.   practice

    B.   winding

    C.   unabridged

    D.   verbose

    E.   concise

134. The capital of that country is a mixture of _luxury_ and...........

    A.   depravity

    B.   decadence

    C.   antiquity

    D.   squalor

    E.   affluence

135. Margaret was _convinced_ that the plan would work, but even after explaining the reasons in detail, her mother remained..............

    A.   annoyed

    B.   sincere

    C.   surprise

    D.   sceptical

    E.   afraid

136. Although Mr. Sanusi was reputed to be partial, his successor was a ………administrator.

    A.   fair

    B.   careless

    C.   corrupt

    D.   wicked

    E.   cruel

137. He has an erratic nature as opposed to his brother who is more…..

    A.   gentle

    B.   predictable

    C.   sombre

    D.   easy-going

    E.   good-mannered.

138. The slothful night guard was replaced with a more……

    A.   devoted

    B.   inactive

    C.   honest

    D.   wise

    E.   diligent

- **CHOOSE THE MOST APPROPRIATE WORD TO FILL IN THE GAP.**

139. If Daddy isn't upstairs, he……..out.

    A. must go

    B. must have gone

    C. will have gone

    D. shall have gone

    E. will have go

140. By the time he returned from exile, his house was in a state of………

    A. deprivation

    B. disturbance

    C. direction

    D. dilapidation

    E. destruction

141. Obi made a resolution to………smoking for two years.

    A. denounce

    B. renounce

    C. repel

    D. reject

    E. refuse.

142. Politicians have to go on constant campaigns to improve their......with the public.

    A.   picture

    B.   portrayal

    C.   image

    D.   illusion

    E.   idea.

143. The officer was accused of.....public funds

    A.   swallowed

    B.   chopping

    C.   embezzling

    D.   forging

    E.   duping

144. Tunde's claim of being at his friend's house on the day of the incident was a perfect …….

    A.   confession

    B.   verdict

    C.   alibi

    D.   case

    E.   justification

145. I never feel comfortable……..on the streets.

    A.   to be eating

    B.   to have eaten

    C.   eating

    D.   to eat

    E.   to eating.

After each of the following sentences, a list of possible interpretations of the sentence is given. *Choose the interpretation that you consider appropriate for each sentence.*

146. The boxer fainted at the end of the second round but they brought him round in no time. This means that they

    A.   brought him home

    B.   brought him out of the ring

    C.   stopped the fight

    D.   treated him and he regained consciousness

    E.   took him round for the spectators to see.

147. She pictures to herself what it might be like to be married to John Lenon.

This means that she

    A.   saw a photograph of herself getting married to John

    B.   imagined her-self married to John

    C.   thought about her marriage to John

    D.   saw a picture of John

E. was thinking about her wedding day.

148. The athlete in lane three has begun to pick up. This means that the athlete has

    A. picked up a baton
    B. led the others
    C. dropped behind
    D. gained some speed
    E. kept abreast with the others.

149. He is dead to all feelings of shame. This means that he

    A. runs away from anything shameful
    B. is shameless
    C. sees shame as death
    D. is shy of anything shameful
    E. feels shame more than any other person.

150. My brother complained that his hands were full.

    A. he carried a heavy load in his hand
    B. he was unwilling to help me.
    C. He was afraid
    D. There was blood on his hands
    E. He was fully occupied.

151. My friend is the crown prince. This means that he

    A. has a crown

    B. wears a crown

    C. is the most popular of all the princes

    D. is the next in succession to the throne.

    E. Will become king after some other ruling houses.

152. The teacher advised the latecomers to take a leaf out of the punctual students' books. This means that the teacher advised the latecomers to

    A. borrow a sheet of paper from the punctual students

    B. lend him their book

    C. borrow books from the punctual students

    D. follow the example given by the punctual students

    E. borrow leafs from the classmates.

153. The military regime trod on may toes in its attempt to wage war against indiscipline. This means it

    A. stepped on many people's feet

    B. walked in a militant manner

    C. conscribed many people into the army

    D. made many improvements

    E. offended many people.

154. As a result of inflation, many families can hardly make ends meet. This means that many families cannot

   A.   move from one end of the town to the other

   B.   meet other families during the weekends

   C.   live within their means

   D.   keep their jobs.

   E.   To go work regularly.

155. The children traded on their mother's generosity. This means that the children

   A.   took advantage of their mother's generosity

   B.   sold their mother's goods because she was generous

   C.   were able to make a profit from their sales.

   D.   Had many admirers because their mother was generous

   E.   Traded with their mother and this made her generous to them.

From the words or group of words lettered A to E below each of the following sentences, *__choose the word or group of words that is nearest in meaning to the underlined word or phrases as it is used in the sentence__*.

156. Janet was presumptuous in sitting for the O/Level last December.

    A. too clever

    B. too presuming

    C. too gifted

    D. to anxious

    E. too self-confident

157. Shade said that her mother was taciturn

    A. did not talk much

    B. talked too much

    C. did not talk brilliantly

    D. talked witlessly

158. Kangwana has always been a dogged fighter for the liberation of his country.

    A. disciplined

    B. weary

    C. compromising

    D. determined

    E. successful

159. The idea is laudable, but this is an inopportune time

    A. a suitable

    B. a wrong

    C. a busy

    D. a good

E. an austere

160. It is a pity that I had no inkling of his plans.

    A. understanding
    B. sign
    C. symptoms
    D. hint
    E. taste

161. Because of some feeling of anxiety he would not believe that all was well.

    A. uncertainty
    B. uneasiness
    C. excitement
    D. abnormality
    E. restlessness

162. Mary has always been painstaking in her pursuits

    A. cruel
    B. thorough
    C. gentle
    D. courageous
    E. generous

163. The appearance of the locusts at that time of the year was regarded as an omen.

    A.   a pest
    B.   a companion
    C.   a sign
    D.   a vision
    E.   a curse

164. A wise man plans his life very carefully.

    A.   tactfully
    B.   officiously
    C.   sincerely
    D.   judiciously
    E.   meticulously

165. Jide's mind was always full of ingenious thoughts

    A.   silly
    B.   shocking
    C.   generous
    D.   useless
    E.   brilliant

from the words or group of words lettered A to D, *choose the word or group of words that best completes each of the following sentences*.

166. The second in command will take....from him when he goes on leave.

    A. up

    B. over

    C. under

    D. out

167. I wonder how much of a worker's salary goes.....food these days.

    A. for

    B. in

    C. into

    D. from

168. The two friends have fallen......with each other.

    A. back

    B. over

    C. off

    D. out

169. The messenger is becoming mentally....so he should see a psychiatrist.

    A. handicapped

    B. balanced

    C. deranged

    D. retarded

170. Yemi is always surrounded by friends anywhere she goes because she is a ....person.

    A. friendless

    B. wise

    C. good

    D. likable

171. Her defence was not............enough, so she had to be convicted.

    A. convincing

    B. well

    C. loud

    D. interesting

172. The doctor could not even lay his hands on a.......to listen to the patient's heart beat.

    A. scalpel

    B. cardiograph

    C. stethoscope

    D. microscope

173. The Dinner dance was too…..so I did not enjoy it.

    A.   interesting

    B.   boring

    C.   enjoyable

    D.   fantastic

174. The project is……..,so we can embark on it.

    A.   inflammable

    B.   palpable

    C.   feasible

    D.   plausible

175. I shouldn't blame him much; I ……..would have made the same mistake.

    A.   myself

    B.   himself

    C.   herself

    D.   itself.

176. They……know the seriousness of the offence they committed.

    A.   ourselves

    B.   theirselves

    C.   themselves

    D.   yourselves.

177. The Director's table is........

    A.   wide about 1.05 metres and long about 1.8 metres

    B.   about 1.05 metres width and 1.8 metres length

    C.   about wide 1.05 metres and long 1.8 metres

    D.   about 1.05 metres wide and 1.8 metres long.

178. The bride clothed herself in a...........

    A.   white beautiful wedding dress

    B.   beautiful white wedding dress

    C.   wedding white beautiful dress

    D.   beautiful white weding dress

179. The new Head of State was escorted to the dance by..........

    A.   young, smartly-dressed, green-uniformed soldiers.

    B.   Smartly-dressed, green-uniformed young soldiers.

    C.   Green-uniformed, smartly-dressed, young soldier

    D.   Young soldiers, smartly-dressed, green-unformed.

180. ....mandate, I drew up a programme of events.

    A.   Having given

    B.   Being given

    C.   Having been given

    D.   Having to give.

181. He decided to return the jacket to………..

   A.   is

   B.   him

   C.   her

   D.   their

182. We ought to have visited the International Trade Fair……….

   A.   haven't we

   B.   can't we

   C.   oughtn't we

   D.   shouldn't we

183. I did……….late to attend the wedding.

   A.   decide

   B.   decided

   C.   took decision

   D.   had to decide

184. Inyang………absent from school for two weeks.

   A.   has

   B.   has been

   C.   will have been

   D.   have been.

185. As a child, I enjoyed..........to stories.

    A.   to listen

    B.   to be listening

    C.   listening

    D.   having listened.

186. The twins loved........so tenderly

    A.   each other

    B.   themselves

    C.   each other's

    D.   one another.

187. The book is not mine; it is

    A.   my brothers

    B.   my brother's

    C.   my brothers'

    D.   of my brother.

188. The manager will not attend the meeting, and his secretary won't....

    A.   rather

    B.   also

    C.   either

    D.   so also

189. There seems……the people can do to improve the economy.

    A. very little

    B. rather little

    C. much little

    D. too little

190. Because of the economic depression….will become jobless.

    A. many more young people

    B. much less your people

    C. much more young people

    D. few more young people.

191. The little orphan was entrusted …….his grandparents.

    A. with

    B. for

    C. at

    D. to

192. The meal was….I asked for more.

    A. very delicious that

    B. so delicious that

    C. that so delicious

    D. too delicious that.

193. Let me have your.....

    A. new blue straw hat

    B. blue new straw hat

    C. straw new blue hat

    D. new straw blue hat.

194. If Ade hadn't broken his leg, he.....won the race.

    A. would

    B. would have

    C. wouldn't have

    D. had.

195. The man said that he saw the thief.....the money.

    A. stole

    B. steal

    C. to steal

    D. to be stealing.

196. After ten years of separation, Mary, James and John met suddenly. They just started at.......

    A. one another

    B. themselves

    C. oneself

    D. each other

197. ………of the twins do you like better?

    A.   who

    B.   whose

    C.   which

    D.   who's

198. She was crying because she was not sure……would care for her fatherless children.

    A.   whom

    B.   who

    C.   which

    D.   whose

199. The man……

    A.   last month only died

    B.   died only last month

    C.   died last only month

    D.   died late only month.

200. You are a member of the club,……..?

    A.   aren't you

    B.   were you

    C.   weren't you

    D.   isn't it

In the following passages the numbered gaps indicate missing words. Against each number in the list below passage five choices are offered lettered **A to E. for each question choose the word that is the most suitable to fill the numbered gap in the passage**.

The –201-contains many kinds of rocks which are mostly used for different kinds of –202-and -203-.removing rock from the -204-is called -205-.. Rocks are either cut out or are blasted –206- with –207-. One method of cutting out the stone is by –208- holes and –209- wedges into them. The stone used in –210- is usually blasted. Some of the most import kinds of rocks are –211-, marble, slate and limestone. These rocks are often not –212- because of the –213- they –214- since they will be used for –125- houses.

	A	B	C	D	E
201.	earth	world	floor	grass	carpet
202.	grinding	stoning	building	wedging	catapulting
203.	erection	obstruction	destruction	construction	blockading
204.	floor	ground	layer	socket	world
205.	digging	excavating	lifting	drilling	quarrying
206.	soft	loose	solid	firm	watery
207.	bombs	acid	erosion	explosives	pumps
208.	breaking	slicing	dissecting	drilling	throwing
209.	drilling	driving	scooping	cultivating	pulling
210.	blockmaking	plastering	roadmaking	roofing	plumbing

211.	gold	iron	tin	aluminum	granite
212.	necessary	appropriate	important	available	eminent
213.	acids	chemicals	spirits	gases	oil
214.	obtain	contain	allow	prevent	present
215.	obstructing	blockading	erecting	destroying	creating

PASSAGE B

A lot of power is needed to run almost all the –216– used in factories and electricity provides this power. Water is the cheapest way of producing this kind of power, which is called –217–. In this –218– some kinds of engines called turbines are used. A let of –219– is needed all round to drive the turbines. This means that a dam must be built to form a big –220–. As a result of this, even in the dry season, there is enough water to rush down the hugh-221- and drive the turbines .The turbines drive the -222-which make the –223-. The Kanji Dam is the biggest dam in Nigeria. There was a narrow -224- to hold the water when the dam was built. There was also the Togo Island in the middle of River Niger which facilitates the building of the dam. It was built at a total –225- of $180 million and it –226- enough electricity to the country and the neighboring country, the Republic of Benin. One –227-advantage is that the kainji dam prevents-228- by -229- the water of the River Niger. It also provides water for –230-some of the dry areas around it.

216. engines   machines   motors   diesels   locomotives

217. hydrocarbon   bydrogrphy   hydromotion   hydromechanics   hydroelectricity

218. arrangement   framework   working   system   setting

219. liquid   oil   water   steam   vapour

220. river   canal   lake   swamp   waterbed

221. hoses   pipe line   tubes   cables   pipes

222. generators   plants   steamers   boilers   rollers

223.	power	electricity	current	electrons	protons
224.	slope	island	valley	hillside	underground
225.	estimate	sum	price	cost	budget
226.	brings	gives	produces	supplies	manufactured
227.	biological	chemical	physical	economical	geographical
228.	flooding	diking	overfilling	overflowing	overreaching
229	shedding	controlling	restraining	constraining	holding
230-.	watering	fertilizing	manuring	irrigating	sprinkling

In each of the following sentences, there is one word underlined and one gap. *From the list of words lettered A to E, choose the word that is most nearly opposite in meaning to the underlined word and that will, correctly fill the gap in the sentence.*

231. Bola has a strong <u>aversion</u> for lying but an…to tell the truth

    A.   inclination

    B.   exception

    C.   example

    D.   interest

    E.   inkling

232. The suspect's sincerely placated the judge while on the other hand the lawyer's arrogance....him.

    A. perplexed

    B. infuriated

    C. embarrassed

    D. hardened

    E. grieved

233. The outgoing prefect had many....and hardly and vices

    A. congratulations

    B. prizes

    C. records

    D. qualities

    E. virtues

234. It is sad when indolent people outnumber the ....ones

    A. hard-working

    B. prudent

    C. trustworthy

    D. devoted

    E. perfect.

235. Thompson's account of the incident was as exhaustive as Mercy's

   A.   interesting

   B.   scanty

   C.   incredible

   D.   thorough

   E.   stilted

236. Although Ada is usually over-dressed, on her wedding day she was…

   A.   ornate

   B.   unadorned

   C.   bedecked

   D.   morose

   E.   ugly

237. He was a novice when he was first employed, but now he is an…….

   A.   idealist

   B.   innovator

   C.   expert

   D.   inventor

   E.   amateur.

238. John was living under the illusion that his father was rich, but when the man dies, John was faced with the ………

    A.   allusion

    B.   vision

    C.   reality

    D.   clarity

    E.   accuracy

239. Uphold honour in all your endeavours, and avoid……….

    A.   disgrace

    B.   unpopularly

    C.   failure

    D.   favour

    E.   poverty

From the words lettered A to E, choose the one that best completes each of the following sentences.

240. He……………….to be a doctor, but whether this is true or not, I do not know.

    A.   protests

    B.   insists

    C.   confesses

    D.   professes

    E.   agrees

241. Ade was asked in his own interest to….the statement he had made.

    A. retrace

    B. contradict

    C. erase

    D. retract

    E. abolish

242. Mary was asked to pay a….of £500.00 before her television set would be repaired.

    A. guarantee

    B. cash

    C. deposit

    D. registration

    E. commission

243. An artist has been …to paint the president portrait

    A. uplifted

    B. drafted

    C. entitled

    D. commissioned

244. With determination they were able to…..the problem.

    A. mount

    B. surpass

    C. surmount

D. attack

245. It would rather be hash to take a....decision on the matter.

    A. head

    B. heady

    C. headstrong

    D. headlong

246. The three rascals finally hit...an excellent plan for entering the castle.

    A. aside
    B. to
    C. upon
    D. by
    E. at

After each of the following sentences, a list of possible interpretations of all or part of the sentence is given. *Choose the interpretation that you consider appropriate for each sentence.*

247. A retrenched worker has no alternative but to tighten his belt if he is to survive. This means that a retrenched worker will have to

    A. wear tight belt

    B. be more prudent in his spending

    C. go without food

    D. slim down a little.

248. It took him two months before, he could find his feet at the new office. This means that he

   A. found his lost foot hold

   B. became an expert in dancing

   C. became used to things

   D. made new friends.

249. When my car was stolen, my friend asked whether it was covered against fire and theft. He was asking whether I

   A. had covering-cloth for it

   B. covered it with fireproof material

   C. put it under lock and key

   D. had it insured

250. Whatever you think, our decision at the meeting stands. This means that the decision

   A. is an order

   B. is a standing order

   C. remains unchanged

   D. was taken standing.

251. After fives minutes of argument, Olu was advised to go and sleep on the issue. This means that Olu

   A. was advised to use the issue as a bed

   B. was advised to go and sleep

   C. was advised to go and take a decision

   D. was advised to go and think it over.

252. Flex has learnt to take his friends' promises with a pinch of salt. This means that he has learnt not to

   A. listen to them without testing his food for salt

   B. rely on what his friends promise

   C. believed that his friends will give his wife some salt

   D. accept salt along with other essential commodities from his friends.

253. The Union said the workers will surely go on strike if they are pushed to the wall. This means that they will on strike if

   A. the factory walls are pulled down

   B. they have no shelter

   C. they have no food

   D. they have no alternative.

254. Tola's remarks were passed with her **tongue in her cheek.** This means that she

    A.   should not be taken seriously

    B.   hid her tongue in her cheeks

    C.   cut her tongue and hid it in her cheek

    D.   passed the remarks to hurt people's feeling

255. I want to keep the matter between you, me and the gatepost. This means that I want us to

    A.   stand by the gatepost to discuss the matter

    B.   keep a distance in discussing the matter

    C.   bring the matter to the notice of people

    D.   keep the matter in strict confidence.

256. Tolu is the black sheep of the family. This means that Tolu is the only

    A.   different child

    B.   disgraceful child

    C.   dark-complexioned child

    D.   useless, good-for-nothing child.

From the words or group of words lettered A to E below each of the following sentences, choose the one that is **nearest in meaning** to the underlined word or words as used in the sentence.

257. Jacob's inordinate ambition led to his downfall

   A.   pleasant

   B.   clever

   C.   desired

   D.   slow

   E.   excessive

258. He often makes out he is ill

   A.   pretends

   B.   writes

   C.   looks as if

   D.   denies

   E.   confirms

259. With the current wave of armed robbery in the country, there is a need for more vigilance.

   A.   care

   B.   courage

   C.   silence

   D.   watchfulness

   E.   sleeplessness

260. The chairman was taken in by his secretary's excuse

    A.   conceived

    B.   released

    C.   deceived

    D.   invited

261. To our chagrin, the accused was freed by the judge

    A.   expectation

    B.   desire

    C.   joy

    D.   disappointment

    E.   prediction.

262. The student was dismissed because of his nefarious deed

    A.   decent

    B.   proud

    C.   naughty

    D.   disobedient

    E.   wicked

263. The enemies could not enter our town because of the barricade

    A.   walls

    B.   hill

    C.   barrier

    D.   barracks

    E.   moat

from the words or group of words lettered A to D, ***choose the words that best complete*** each of the following sentences.

264. I have been told that, when I was a child, I was a......

    A. many little fellow

    B. little manly fellow

    C. fellow many little

    D. fellow little manly.

265. When I received my first pay, I bought myself a.......... shirt.

    A. green new cotton

    B. new cotton green

    C. new green cotton

    D. green cotton new

266. One thing we can say for sure is....about this crazy April fool game plan.

    A. mother's getting angry

    B. mother angry getting

    C. mother to be getting angry

    D. mother getting angry.

267. Mr. Alaba is the chairman of the ....disciplinary committee appointed by the principal.

    A. three-man

    B. three-men

    C. three-man's

D. three-man's

268. The senior prefect did not know….the invited guest at the gate.

   A. that he should see
   B. that he can met
   C. that he met
   D. to have met.

269. The prices of commodities …..since last year.

   A. have gone up
   B. has gone up
   C. will have gone up
   D. went up

270. He was sure…..

   A. in their success
   B. for the success
   C. of their success
   D. for their succession

271. The reason for…was not given

   A. his dismiss
   B. his dismissed
   C. his dismissal
   D. the dismissed

272. Take the money from ....it.

    A. whomever offers

    B. whichever offers

    C. whichsoever offers

    D. whoever offers

273. The principal has gone to Ibadan and will come back in.....time.

    A. two weeks

    B. two's week

    C. two week's

    D. two weeks'

274. Salt is....in demand at the market.

    A. very much

    B. very

    C. very more

    D. very most

275. Many of us wept when we got to the.......of the accident.

    A. site

    B. area

    C. sight

    D. scene

276. The government has ordered.....into the recent student demonstration in the country.

   A. the probe

   B. a trial

   C. a probe

   D. the trial

277. He was arrested on......of stealing

   A. the grounding

   B. ground

   C. a ground

   D. the grounds

278. Having failed in his first attempt, he wants to have ……..

   A. Re- trial

   B. a trial

   C. a try

   D. another try

279. Nike's mother instructed her to add …….salt to the soup

   A. a few more

   B. a little more

   C. some few

   D. many more

280. The …..model was the best of them all

    A. fair-skinned, beautiful Ghanaian

    B. Ghanaian, beautiful fair-skinned

    C. Beautiful, fair-skinned Ghanaian

    D. Fair-skinned, Ghanaian beautiful.

281. ……..rather remain a loyal citizen

    A. I'd

    B. I'll

    C. Would

    D. Should

282. My sister bought…….bag

    A. an expensive, very attractive synthetic

    B. a very attractive synthetic expensive

    C. a very expensive and attractive, synthetic

    D. an expensive and attractive, very synthetic.

283. Bring that book,……mine

    A. its

    B. he's

    C. it's

    D. it

284. ....the present circumstances, I think we have to retrace our steps.

   A.   with

   B.   by

   C.   in

   D.   at

285. The quality of food in the boarding school has started to go....

   A.   off

   B.   out

   C.   down

   D.   back

286. To award scholarships to students now is......impossible.

   A.   exactly

   B.   virtually

   C.   accurately

   D.   normally

287. .....we have worked hard, we should be promoted this year.

   A.   despite

   B.   although

   C.   however

   D.   since

288. His suggestions are irrelevant …..the discussion

    A.   at

    B.   for

    C.   to

    D.   with

289. If………a raincoat, we should not have been drenched

    A.   we have had

    B.   we have been having

    C.   we had had

    D.   we were having

290. Before the bus arrived passengers…..for a long time

    A.   have been waiting

    B.   had being waiting

    C.   have waited

    D.   had waited

291. ……I shall not be able to write you a letter

    A.   until I hear from you

    B.   until after I hear from you

    C.   never until I hear from you

    D.   not until I hear from you.

292. You aren't going home,…….

    A.   weren't you?

    B.   Isn't it?

    C.   Are you?

    D.   Is it?

USE OF ENGLISH

COMPREHENSION

Read each passage carefully and answer the questions that follow.

PASSAGE 1

Our planet is at risk. Our environment is under threat. The air we breathe, the water we drink, the seas we fish in, the soils we farm, the forests, animals and plants which surround us are in danger. New terms and words describe these problems – acid rain, the green house effect, global warming, holes in the ozone layer, desertification and industrial pollution. We are changing our environment. More and more gases and wastes escape from our factories. Rubbish, oil spillages and detergents damage our rivers and seas. Forests give us timber and paper, but their loss results in soil erosion and also endangers wildlife.

The richer countries of the world are mainly responsible for industrial pollution. This is where most of all the commercial energy is produced. In developing countries poverty causes people to change their environment – to overgraze grasslands, to cut down trees for new land and firewood, to farm poor soil for food.

The United Nations Environmental Protection Agency says that an area of forest the size of Sierra Leone disappear every year. Trees are cut down for timber which is used for building, furniture, paper and fuel. They are also destroyed to provide land on which to graze animals and build new villages and towns. But trees have many other important uses. Trees protect the land from heavy downpour of rain and their roots help to hold the soil together. Forest contains one fifth of all the species of birds in the world. In our forests, there may be plants and animals which could help in the discovery of new medicines or crops.

To rescue and conserve our beautiful world, we must act cooperatively. Individuals, communities, nations and learning to protect the natural environment, we can manage the earth's resources for generations to come.

293. The risk referred to in the passage is

    A.   environmental induced

    B.   industrially produced

    C.   man-made

    D.   sociologically produced.

294. From the passage, it can be deduced that the inhabitants of developing countries

    A.   take more care of their environment than those in developed countries

    B.   generate more harmful industrial by-products

    C.   degrade the environment to eke out a livelihood

    D.   cut down trees only for farmlands and fuel.

295. According to the passage, the size of forest depleted annually is

    A.   minimal

    B.   colossal

C. infinitesimal

D. infinite

296. The writer holds the richer countries responsible for industrial pollution because of their

    A. technological innovation

    B. energy requirements

    C. industrial revolution

    D. lack of interest in environmental protection.

297. The message of the writer is the

    A. need for the developed countries to assist the poorer ones

    B. grave dangers of global warming

    C. urgent need to protect the natural environment

    D. need to research into other uses of the trees in our forests.

PASSAGE II

If economists were a bit more modest, they would admit that no one knows exactly how many Nigerians there are. The National Population Bureau estimated that there would be 116 million in 1986, but this figure was derived from projections based on the much disputed figures of the 1963 census, using an annual population growth rate that was at best a guess work. Notwithstanding, that the margin of error could be as large as plus or minus 20 million, economists have still felt confident to speak of Nigeria's per capital income, birth and mortality rates, literacy rates and so on, as if they were quoting precise figures.

So much in Nigeria is determined on the basis of population that the lack of accurate figures has a significant adverse effect on policies. One obviously affected area is development planning, which for the lack of reliable data, frequently looks like an exercise in futility. An example of what happens is the country's Universal Primary Education (UPE) scheme launched in 1976. Policy makers had expected, on the basis of the 1975/76 primary school enrolment of just under 5 million that they would not have to cope with much more than 6 million school children in the first year. But the enrolment in 1976/77 turned out to be 8.4 million rising to 10.1 million the following year. The unanticipated cost of catering for the larger number was the main cause of the collapse of the worthy scheme after only four years.

Population also plays an important role in revenue allocation, specifically in the sharing of the states' portion of the Federal Account, some percentage of which is based on population or population-related factors. Because of the contentious nature of the subject, the compromise has been to use estimates based on the 1963 census figures, even when such a move produced ridiculous situations. It is for all these reasons that the Babangida Administration's effort to ascertain the nation's population is such a worthwhile venture.

298. It would be more realistic of economist to

    A.   accept the unreliability of Nigeria's census figures

    B.   ascertain how many Nigerian there are

    C.   discard the disputed 1963 census figures

    D.   accept marginal errors in the census figures

299. Precise national population figures are required in order to

    A.   know the number of people to cater for in the Universal Primary Education programme

    B.   be able to undertake proper implementation of governmental policies

    C.   avert unanticipated expenditure

    D.   be able to speak of population statistics with confidence

300. The contentious nature of the subject refers to

    A.   the population

    B.   the disputed 1963 census figures

    C.   development planning

    D.   revenue allocation.

301. The reference to 'Universal Primary Education' in this passage is significant because it shows

    A.   why the census figures were disputed

    B.   the failure and collapse of the programme

    C.   the misleading effect of unreliable information

    D.   how a worthy scheme could be made worthless by poor planning strategies.

302. As far as the solution to the population problem of Nigeria is concerned, the writer of this passage is

    A.   optimistic

    B.   pessimistic

    C.   indifferent

    D.   disturbed

PASSAGE III

Let's begin with a picture

He must not have been more than thirty years old. The oval face, devoid of those wrinkles of age, the well-turfed and black hair, and his still complete though brown set of teeth supported this assessment. All he had for clothing was a piece of cloth with some words written on it. It must have been one of those cloth-posters used but now abandoned by 'show-biz' promoters. Across his neck was yet another cloth which is more Nigerian national colours of green and white. His feet were naked-just as they came from their creator. In one hand he had an empty tin. He talked ceaselessly and in a disordered fashion. The other free hand emphasized his spoken words and gestures. As he talked, he gazed at you as if you were responsible for this pathetic condition. He looked redeemable, though. There are many of his type in various urban centers.

Beggars! They are in every conceivable place. At the bank, the supermarket, the church, the mosque, the post office- there you will meet them. Before you know it, the more healthy ones besiege you for alms almost to the point of assault. Surely, there is no rationale in giving alms to someone who is physically stronger than you are and who, from all indication, can and should work and fend for himself. Some others are feeble and unfortunately handicapped. Women and young girls constitute a sizeable number of these healthy beggars. Some are nursing mothers and one wonders who their husbands are. Conception by Mr. Nobody, perhaps. The young girls in this category are the mother-beggars of tomorrow. But tell me can't the society be spared this human waste?

303. The writer is describing a

    A.   picture

    B.   man

    C.   picture of a man

    D.   man and a picture

304. '……this assessment' refers to the man's

    A.   face

    B.   hair

    C.   age

    D.   naked feet

305. 'Beggars' in the context of the first line of the third paragraph is a

    A.   phrase

    B.   sentence

    C.   noun

    D.   modifier

306. The human waste referred to by the writer is brought about by

    A.   over feeding

    B.   the irresponsible men who put female beggars in the family way

    C.   the mother-beggars of tomorrow

    D.   the society

307. An appropriate title for the passage is

    A.   A picture, the young man and female beggars

    B.   Destitute in the society

    C.   The problems of mad people in the society

    D.   Young men and medicants

LEXIS AND STRUCTURE

Use the passage below to answer questions 308 to 317. The passage has gaps numbered 308 to 317. Immediately following each gap, four options are provided. *Choose the appropriate option for each gap.*

In addition to further reading as a vital arm of referencing, the use of the dictionary in language learning should be emphasized. It cannot be denied that dictionaries do supply facts about a language which may be difficult to find anywhere else.

308 (A. Information B. Words C. Details D. Knowledge) about grammar, usage, status, derivation and so on necessary for comprehension are contained in the dictionary. While context, word analysis and synonym search contribute immensely to the 309 (A. forming B. getting C. knowing D. creation) of meaning, an efficient use of the dictionary to enrich the experimental conceptual background to create a menacing context cannot be denied. The 310 (A. possession B. fact C. use D. employment) of both the specialist and general dictionaries should be encouraged as the case may be. Not that students should jeopardize reading fluency by 311 (A. considering B. pondering C. mediating D. looking up) every word that they do not understand, rather in their bid to read chunks or groups of words in a text, lexical items that 312 (A. may B. Will C. can D. shall) obstruct meaning may be quickly checked up in the dictionary. Glossing over a word or I guessing through context may not be sufficient. 313 (A.

practice B. exercise C. notes D. passages) to encourage the use of the dictionary as an aid to reading and a tool for checking words used in writing must be built 314 (A on to B. in C. into D. unto) the reading text. This skill can be easily transferred to the students' subject areas as well. A barrage of criticism, like: students' excessive reliance on the dictionary instead of contextual 315 (A. reading B. meaning C. decoding D. guessing), reduction in the speed of reading, time wastage and so on abound against students' use of the dictionary when reading. It may however be argued that 316 (A. asking B. teaching C. making D. allowing) students to guess the meaning of words from context and then compares this with the dictionary entry for such words is a discovery 317 (A. procedure B. method C. means D. strategy) for enlarging the conceptual environment and vision of students on the various interpretations that may be given to a word.

In each of these questions, choose the option opposite in meaning to the words in italics.

318. Ojo's response infuriated his wife

    A.   annoyed

    B.   pleased

    C.   surprised

    D.   confused

319 He accepted a mundane task without hesitation

   A.   great

   B.   lowly

   C.   menial

   D.   moderate

320 It is a unique opportunity for her to demonstrate the reality of her faith

   A.   strange

   B.   usual

   C.   golden

   D.   intimacy

321. Her identification with the king is publicly known

   A.   hatred

   B.   disassociation

   C.   relationship

   D.   intimacy

322. The economic situation in the country is obviously gloomy

   A.   encouraging

   B.   moody

   C.   unknown

   D.   regrettable

323. One wonders if the situation will improve

    A. brighten

    B. diminish

    C. disintegrate

    D. worsen

324. Language teachers believe that grammar exercise stretch the mind

    A. expand

    B. ruin

    C. enrich

    D. restrict

325. These two books are identical

    A. alike

    B. similar

    C. different

    D. equal

326. The doctor tried to alleviate his patient's pain

    A. relieve

    B. worsen

    C. kill

    D. cure

327. The instructions on the examination paper are explicit

    A. simple

    B. ambiguous

    C. detailed

    D. definite

328. Okoro is an amateur wrestler

    A. skilful

    B. good

    C. professional

    D. strong

In each of question 329 to 346 **choose the option nearest in meaning to the word(s) or phrase(s) in italics.**

329. If your life is in turmoil, always take courage

    A. devastation

    B. crisis

    C. trial

    D. tragedy

330. Do you know one of the most astounding events of my life?

    A. special

    B. amazing

    C. serious

    D. outstanding

331. Adeniji is suffering from the consequences of alienation

    A. confinement

    B. isolation

    C. enclosure

    D. imprisonment

332. The terms of the contract stuck in my throat

    A. were beyond me

    B. were not clear

    C. were ambiguous

    D. became obsolete

333. He was asked to give copious examples to appear convincing

   A. concrete

   B. rigid

   C. cogent

   D. many

334. Some children mimic their teachers

   A. imitate

   B. mime

   C. ridicule

   D. tease

335. He works long hours collecting trash to eke out a livelihood.

   A. try a living

   B. struggle for a living

   C. make a living

   D. carve out a living

336. Everybody complained of a lean harvest last year.

   A. surplus

   B. abundant

   C. poor

   D. thin

337. He is very modest in his demands

    A. honest

    B. bogus

    C. extravagant

    D. humble

338. The patient disregarded the advice of the doctor.

    A. ignored

    B. disobeyed

    C. questioned

    D. respected

339. The newly elected leader has pledged to ensure better life for the citizens.

    A. vowed

    B. agreed

    C. undertaken

    D. undertaking

340. Statesman are revered for their objectivity

    A. referred

    B. respected

    C. remembered

    D. rejected

341. He has been advised to keep his head, the crisis notwithstanding.

    A. avoid being beaten or insulted

    B. keep calm

    C. save his head

    D. prevent being beheaded

342. The police ran the criminal to earth

    A. jailed him

    B. knocked him down

    C. discovered him

    D. buried him

343. Garbs always puts his shoulder to the wheel.

    A. sits with his shoulders straight when he is driving

    B. works energetically at the task in hand

    C. performs tasks assigned him grudgingly

    D. holds the steering wheel firmly when he is driving

344. He reneged on the agreement between him and his employees

    A. kept

    B. failed to keep

    C. failed to approve

    D. failed to sign

345. He is cradulous

    A. ordible

    B. creditable

    C. gullible

    D. fallible

346. The company has gone under.

    A. suffered some loss

    B. broken up

    C. become broke

    D. become bankrupt

In each of questions 347 to 387 *fill each gap with the appropriate option from the list following the gap.*

347. Many people believe that nuclear power will solve our energy problems (A. indeed B. But C. however D. on the contrary), this has not been prove to be true.

348. ……(A. conclusively B. to conclude C. in conclusion D. the conclusion), sign post words are useful to reader.

349. Every programming language and software package ……..(A. have its B. have their C. has its D. has their limitation).

350. A programme of good exercise may help a person fight…(A. out B. at C. with D. off) cold.

351. Baba and…. (A. him B. His C. he D. he's) participated in the tournament.

352. It was …..(A. they B. them C. those D. theirs) who fought the civil war.

353. The physicians have more people in…..waiting rooms than…..(A. his/he B. there/they C. their/they D. them/they) have ever had.

354. Before mechanization, workers ….(A. wring B. wrung C. wrang D. wringed) water out of fabrics with their hand.

355. Four engineers ……(A. worked B. are working C. had worked D. have been working) on this system since March.

356. Having worked all night, the security man…(A. had felt B. felt C. is feeling D. has felt) a sense of accomplishment.

357. Three quarters of the Physics class....(A. improve B. improved C. are improving D. is improving) dramatically.

358. A number of students.....(A. is B. has C. have D. do) missed the opportunity to re-register.

359. It seems to be a well thought.....(A. over B. out C. off D. into) scheme

360. Adekunle is prepared for a ....A. show-off B. show-down C. show-out D. showup) with his opponent following his defeat last season.

361. Tosin refused to be....(A. sad B. placated C. frustrated D. indifference) though he has written the same examination three times.

362. On his....(A. assumption B. ascension C. acceptance D. appointment) of office, the new president announced some drastic measures.

363. The ...was filed .....(A. suit/in B. case/in C. suit/at D. case/at) the Ilorin Magistrate Court.

364. The plaintiff .....(A. asked B. begged C. demanded D. praryed) the court to restrain the defendant from further action

365. My experience in Lagos last week was.....(A. something . B. to excite B. nothing to explain at home C. nothing to write home D. something to celebrate) about.

366. ....(A. had I seen B. have I seen C. should I see D. if I say) him around, I would have informed you.

367. Ahmed is one of the boys who always...(A. does B. would do C. do D. done) good work.

368. I sent....(A. a parcel of B. a flash of C. an item of D. a number of) news to the press yesterday.

369. The university has a large collection of sporting .....(A. equipment B. equipments C. costumes D. aids).

370. He keeps his....(A. surroundings B. surrounding C. premise D. environments) clean always.

371. She has a set of gold....(A. earing B. earings C. earrings D. ear-ring).

372. I have stopped writing letters of application because I ......(A. have heard B. had heard C. heard D. hear) that all the vacancies are filled.

373. A survey of opinions on how pupils feel about their teachers.........(A. had been B. have been C. are being D. has been carried out.

374. The police are looking for.....(A. two big cares black B. two cars big black C. two big black cars D. two black big cars).

375. Adaobi is contemptuous .....(A. to B. at C. for D. of) dishonest people.

376. My goats are grazing ....(A. on B. in C. at D. into) the field.

377. It.....(A. would be B. would have been C. would had been D. will be) easier if he told us himself.

378. Our principal and chairman of the occasion.....(A. has B. having C. have D. had) just arrived.

379. From 7a.m. to 9a.m., he....(A. kept busy serving B. keeps busy to serve C. is busied serving D. kept busy to serve) hot chocolate, often not having time for his own breakfast.

92

380. One of the .....(A. school of thought suggests B. schools of thought suggest C. school of thoughts suggested D. school of thought suggest) selective marking of errors.

You avoid facing .....(A. at B. up C. to D. on to) the reality of life

381. In....(A. more deeper sense B. a much deeper sense c. a most deeper sense D much more deeper sense) we, as politicians, are identified with the masses.

382. In addition, their comments are vague and abstract,...(A. which students find it B. and students find it C. so students find them D. but students find them) difficult to interpret.

383. We are..... to receive your letter and to know that you are ....(A. happy/in good health B. grateful/sound C. pleased/all well D. appreciated/swimming in good health).

384. people who live by....(A. each other known B. one another know C. oneself knows D. themselves know) what loneliness is like.

385. It has been confirmed that the elections.....(A. will be B. is being C. has been D. have being) held in July.

386. The choice to go to the university or not is.....(A. yours' B. your C. yours D. your's)

In each of questions 387 *to select the option A to D that best explains the information conveyed in the sentence*.

387. People may not pick flowers in this park.

    A. people can pick flowers in this park

    B. people may not wish to pick flowers in this park

    C. people are prohibited from picking flowers in this park

    D. people cannot pick flowers from this park.

388. Tom ought not to have told me.

    A. Tom did not tell me but he should

    B. Perhaps Tom was wrong to have told me

    C. Tom told me but it was wrong of him

    D. It was necessary for Tom not to tell me.

389. He can't be swimming all day

    A. It's possible he is not swimming now

    B. It's very likely he is swimming now

    C. He does not have the ability to swim all day

    D. He would not like to swim all day

390. Bolade would make a mess of cooking the rice.

    A. it was typical of Bolade to make a mess of things

    B. Bolade cannot cook

    C. Bolade will not cook the rice well

    D. Bolade does not like cooking rice

391 If I were the captain, I would have led the team to victory

    A.   I was not the captain but I led the team to victory

    B.   I was the captain but I did not lead the team to victory

    C.   I was not the captain and I did not lead the team to victory

    D.   I was the captain and I led the team to victory.

TEST OF ENGLISH

COMPREHENSION

Read the passage carefully and answer the questions that follow.

PASSAGE I

My friend worked with Guinness Brewery in Lagos. Because Bola hails from Efon-Alaye, he was nicknamed 'City'. City and I became fond of each other after my first ordeal. Both of us sat mute at a dual desk from the first day in school. Soon, we were given what our teacher called a diagnostic test meant as a yardstick for ability grouping. As luck would have it, he unilaterally, as it were, decided to administer an arithmetic test. Tears rolled down my cheeks as I search nervously for my ball-point pen. Bola apparently filled with pity whispered, 'Tope'. I looked sideways almost blind with tears and he pushed a ball-point pen into my trembling hand. I became more confused. He then whispered a few answers which I copied. In the end, I 'passed and was placed in Bola's group. Henceforth, I became his inseparable 'junior partner'.

In 1961, he went into the Government Trade Centre in Osogbo while I was condemned to living with my uncle in Lagos. Then we lost contact.

One morning in July, 1974, I went to visit him in his office. As he saw me from a distance, he thundered, "Falakua" (my surname is Falana), 'Back from England?" 'From Canada', I said softly. He took me to his office where he pushed a one-pint bottle of stout into my hand but because I couldn't convince him to the contrary, I had what was my first-ever bottle of alcohol. Within two minutes, according to 'the law' that guided the drinking of beer in the brewery, I had gulped two pints down my throat. Suddenly, the whole factory started to spin violently. At 2.00p.m., I staggered out of the factory premises and jumped into a waiting bus....

The bus conductor's hawking shout, 'Saint Agnes' woke me up. I looked at my watch, it was half pass eight. I got up and took some feeble steps out of the bus into the darkness. The bus conductor and the driver laughed at me without asking for the fare. I felt an angry shame as I plodded my weary way home, in the rain.

392. The writer sobbed because

   A. he hated the teacher

   B. he had no ball-point pen

   C. he did not like arithmetic

   D. he was confused by the teacher.

393. What does the statement, 'in the end, I 'passed' connote?

   A. I did not actually pass the test on my own

   B. I passed the test very well

   C. I passed the test after crying

   D. I passed the test after many attempts.

394. Why did the factory spin violently?

    A.   there was a terrible storm

    B.   the writer was tipsy

    C.   the writer was in a bus passing by the factory

    D.   the buildings were falling down.

395 The writer was angry because

    A.   the conductor shouted at him

    B.   the conductor and the driver laughed at him

    C.   it was dark and raining

    D.   he was ashamed of his own behaviour

396. 'I plodded my weary way home' means that I

    A.   walked through the muddy road

    B.   was too weak to walk home

    C.   walked home in weak and tired steps

    D.   was unhappy to go home in the rain.

PASSAGE II

When I first discovered Chip, the mammoth, he was using his extraordinary skill as a tugger in the Great Northern Forest. His owner would simply tap on Chip's tusks for the total number of trees he wanted the creature to gather, then tug his tail. If ten taps were applied to his tusks, Chip would not stop working until he had collected ten trees. I suggested to his owner that it might be to everyone's advantage if Chip's remarkable memory were adapted to other uses. I offered to train him myself; by tapping two numbers – one on each tusk- and then tugging his tail. I planned to teach him the art of multiplication. We worked together, night and day for almost a year and Chip's instruction was almost compete when suddenly I received an urgent request for his services.

We arrived at a local restaurant where a dispute had arisen over a bill. It appeared that the waiter and served a seven fixed price meal to one particular table but had incorrectly calculated the total. Here indeed was the chance I had been waiting for during months of laborious training.

The dinner looked on skeptically as i requested one of them to tap the fixed price on one of Chip's tusks, the restaurant owner tapped the number of meals on the other and then tugged his tail. Chip stood for a few moment and set off for some nearby woods.

As I had anticipated, the animal gave exactly the right answer, but to my great dismay, he did it in tree trunks, thereby leveling the restaurant and three adjoining structures. After much deliberation, I reluctantly parted with him because of the dangers of dealing with large numbers.

397. Chip was a unique creature because of his

    A.   physical ability

    B.   mental ability

    C.   tusks and tail

    D.   huge frame

398. Chip's tail was tugged as

    A.   a sign for him to lift logs

    B.   a sign for him to supply answers to questions

    C.   the only means of destroying the restaurant

    D.   a sign for him to destroy the restaurant

399. The writer taught Chip the art of multiplication by

    A.   tapping one tusk and then the other tusk and finally tugging his tail

    B.   tugging his tail and tusks

    C.   tugging his tail and then tapping his tusks intermittently

    D.   tapping one tail and then the other tail and finally tugging his tusks.

400. 'Here indeed was the chance I had been waiting for'. 'The chance' was to

    A.   show Chip to the people

    B.   calculate painlessly

    C.   put Chip's multiplication art into practice

    D.   test Chip's memory

401. The danger Chip's trainer envisaged for Chip was that he

    A.   could kill anybody

    B.   might destroy more buildings

    C.   might raid more structures for logs

    D.   might level the people around in their buildings.

PASSAGE III

Much hostility towards computers has been based on the fear of widespread unemployment resulting from their introduction. One of the earliest examples of this was the burning of Jacquard's punched-card-operated looms by some weavers in Lyons. Computers are often installed as part of automated production process requiring a minimum of operators, resulting in the loss of many jobs. This has happened, for example, in any steelworks. On the other hand, computers do create jobs. These are more skilled and better paid, though fewer in number than those they replace. Many activities could not continue in their present form without computers, no matter how many people were employed. Examples are the cheque-clearing system of major banks and weather-forecasting. When a firm introduce computers, a few people are usually employed in keep posts such as operators, programmers and data preparations staff. After the new system has settled down, people in non-computer jobs are not always replaced when they leave, resulting in a decrease in the number of employees. This decrease is sometimes offset by a substantial increase in the activity of the firm, resulting from the introduction of computers.

The attitudes of trade unions to computers vary. There is fear of widespread unemployment, and of the takeover of many jobs by computer-trained workers, making promotion for older workers not skilled in the use of computers more difficult. On the other hand, many trade unionists see the drift towards computers as inevitable. They feel their contribution to greater efficiency and productivity will improve the condition of the whole economy.

402. The theme of the first paragraph of this passage is

   A. hostility towards computers

   B. burning of Jacquard's punched-cards-operated looms

   C. unemployment resulting from computerized systems

   D. computers and the fears they create.

403. According to the passage, the introduction of computers is

   A. meant to create unemployment

   B. a response to the growing complexity of modern business

   C. to help provide jobs for few, well-trained profession

   D. to facilitate cheque clearing and weather forecasting.

404. The advantage of computers is that they

   A. make jobs readily available

   B. make all workers more professional

   C. enhance productivity and efficiency

   D. make work more automated and complex

405. According to the passage, in an organization without computers

   A. all types of work are performed manually

   B. less people are employed with more pay

   C. more people are employ with more pay

   D. there is considerable increase in its output.

406. The attitude of trade unions to computers vary because the computer

      A.   is complex

      B.   is a mixed blessing

      C.   has a negative impact

      D.   contributes to greater efficiency

LEXIS AND STRUCTURE

Use the passage below to answer questions 407 to .... the passage has gaps numbered 407 to .... Immediately following each gap, four options are provided. ***Choose the appropriate option for each gap***.

The importance of literacy has for long been recognized and very well expressed 407 (A. but. B. however C. equally D. moreover), of strong fascination and excitement are the value of books and their role in 408 (A. assuaging B. preserving C. ameliorating D. aggravating) knowledge and enhancing the literate tradition. Regrettably, such 409 (A. judgments B. measurements C. appraisals D. valuations) have obviously taken for granted the painstaking process of book 410 (A. evaluation B. development C. artistry D. penmanship), matters of editorial concern, and finally, the dual processes of book design and printing.

We can confidently claim that without printing, not much 411 (A. will have been known B. shall have been known C. would have been known D. should be known) about the past and even 412 (A. fashionable B. simultaneous C. immediate D. contemporary) level of literacy would have been adversely hampered. Without doubt, the role and influence of authors in the advancement of learning 413 (A. shall have been B. would have been C. will have been D. may have been) restricted.

The advent of printing has eliminated the above problems but it has 414 (A. in the process B. on the process C. by the process D. of the process) created its own problems somewhat inadvertently. Perhaps, it is more generous to say that the problems of printing are 415 (A. inherent B. innate C. inbred D. alike) in all developing nations. 416 Good or bad it may seem (A. developing nations, B Developed country C develop nationals D developed cities.) among others has their fair share of the blame as mistakes are synonymous with humans abilities ,no one is perfect.

In each of questions 417 to .., *fill each gap with the appropriate option from the list following the gap*

417. Even….(A. as B. although C. then D. though) things are bad, we must not give up hope.

418. Chrismas is the season for expressing….(A. complement B. compliment C. complements D. compliments).

419. The ball (A shot B. shout C. shott D. kicked) through the shattered windows ,what a skillful mid-fielder.!

420. Hardly had he gone….(A. when B. than C. and D. as) she came in.

421. I…..(A. use to B am used to C. used to D. am use to) do it.

422. He was not….(A. a particular and attentively B. an attentively and particular C. a particularly attentive D. an attentively and particular) person.

423. The cats are friendly but the kitten…..(A. could B. is C. are D. were) not.

424. The….(A. stationeries B. stationeries C. stationery D. stationary) I need are a pen, pencils, erasers, ink and exercise books.

425. If I were in Sweden, I…(A. would B. shall C. can . D. will) be glad.

426. If it.....(A. were B. is C. has D. had) to rain, we will be wet.

427. Being a man of steady means...(A. and, B. perhaps C. with D. at) experience you can rely on his judgment.

428. ....(A. has B. were C. should D. have) he to reveal his secrets, that house would collapse in shame.

429. All....(A. has agree B. having agreed C. have agreed D. have agree) that the date should be changed.

430. Fatima is an adherent ...(A. for B. with C. of D. in) the never –do-well- party.

431. .....(A. Between I and you B. between you and I C. between me and you D. between you and me) there is no love lost.

432. Have you found the solution....(A. to B. on C. for D. about) the problem?

433. The teacher praised him....(A. with B. of C. for D. against) his hard work.

434. Adigwu cannot write....(A. as good B. as well C. good D. gained) as I had thought.

435. Last year, the company...(A. secured B. acquired C. incurred D. gained) a huge debt.

436. The striking students refused...(A. attend B. to be attending C. to attend D. attended) classes.

437. My brother....(A. almost never B. scarcely never C. never more D. hardly ever) comes to see me now.

438. Maradona played....(A. worse B. more worse C. worst D. had than) anyone.

439. My daughter bought...(A. and interesting new story English B. an interesting new English story C. can English new interesting story D. a new interesting English story) book.

440. The thief ....(A. run off B. made off C. charge off D. started off) with her car.

441. Your sister is happy when she ...(A. singe B. sang C. song D. sings).

442. The political party (A. are B. were C. is D. was) formed two years ago.

443. He gave her (A. a bundle B a. pile C.a heap D. a bunch) of flowers.

444. Give me (A. a book B. that book C. this book D. those book) on your desk, please.

445. Chioma Laide (A. sew B. sews C. sewing D. sewn) some clothe.

446. The poor boy lost the prize (A. he had won it, B. he have won it C. he has won D. he had won).

447. The principal furiously demanded (A. us to leave B. that we should leave C. us that we should leave D. to us that we should leave).

448. When she saw us standing by the gate, Jamila asked (A. were we ready? B. if we are ready C. if we ready D. if we were ready?).

449. If you have problems, why not ask your uncle for (A. some advice B. some advices C. advices).

450. Good parents should (A. blame B. fight C. accuse D. rebuke) their children when they misbehave.

451. At the police station, Etim (A. refused B. declined C. denied D. denounced) that he had gone near the place.

452. After much questioning, the police (A. selected B. extracted C. elicited D. exposed) the information they wanted from the suspect.

453. The teacher told his students to open their books (A. to B. on C. at D. in) page forty.

454. On my way to Abuja, I saw a (A. fatal B. disastrous C. ghastly D dangerous) motor accident in which a man sustained serious injuries on his head.

455. An (A. accountable B. uncountable C. unaccountable D. countable) noun usually has no plural form.

456. The carpenter (A. plained B planned C. plaited D. planned) the wood thoroughly

457. the climate of this place is not congenital (A. to B. for C. with D. from) my health.

458. She can run (A. fast B. more faster C. much fast D. faster) than any of you.

459. The suspect was charged (A. for B. as C. on D. with) house breaking.

460. She needs a lot of money to spend during her (A. ten-day leave B. ten-day's leave C. tend day leave D. ten-days' leave).

461. You don't drink tea with milk, do you? (A. no, I do B. No I don't C. no, you don't D. yes, I don't)

462. The Administrator's wife is....of top brands. (A. a designer B exemplar C. an example D. a duplicate).

In each of questions 463 to 4.. *choose the option nearest in meaning to the word(s) or phrase(s) in italics.*

463. He is determined to rule his subjects as a good king

    A.   chief

    B.   leader

    C.   dictator

    D.   monarch

464. Always verify your information before taking action

    A.   check

    B.   establish

    C.   inquire

    D.   consider

465. The troops surrendered to the rival forces

    A.   gave up

    B.   gave in

    C.   gave way

    D.   gave out

466. Do not shirk your responsibilities

    A.   deny

B. accept

C. pass

D. avoid

467. The chief is a connoisseur of antique furniture.

   A. person with terrible judgement

   B. carpenter with good temper

   C. collector of antiques

   D. person with good judgement on matters of taste

468. She would be sent into raptures over this story

   A. be extremely sad

   B. be full of joy and enthusiasm

   C. jump to the sky

   D. collapse

469. Tade is a man of straw

   A. a very important man

   B. an insubstantial person

   C. a man undertaking a financial commitment with adequate means

   D. a man who walk about with a hat

470. Musa's jokes were over ten top

   A. exuberant

   B. interesting and wry

   C. right jokes for the right situation

   D. beyond reasonable limits

471. He was an eminent judge

    A. regular

    B. distinguished

    C. notorious

    D. corrupt

472. One of these fine days, I will be in Jos.

    A. at some time in the future

    B. when the weather is clear

    C. when I am rich

    D. as soon as I am well

473. Ada cut a dash at the party

    A. had a striking appearance

    B. met a handsome man

    C. spent a short time

    D. received a beautiful present.

474. Empathy is one of the attributes of a nurse

    A. encouraging patients

    B. caring for patients

    C. sharing one's feelings

    D. showing acts of kindness.

475. There are several inscrutable circumstances in human life.

    A. unscrupulous

    B. unwholesome

    C. unfathomable

    D. unimaginable

476. The handsome man had a specious appearance.

    A. dazzling

    B. special

    C. sombre

    D. deceptive

477. The accused used very cunning tricks to dupe the bank

    A. careful

    B. old

    C. crafty

    D. insulting

478. The sympathiser's message was profound

    A. superficial

    B. deep

    C. genuine

    D. humane

479. At the reception, Bintu was a real sight for sore eyes.

    A. looked beautiful

    B. looked ugly

    C. dressed offensively

    D. needed eye-treatment.

480. The threat to life on our roads is increasing

    A. danger

    B. risk

    C. menace

    D. peril

481. The fantastic Atilogu Dancers from Nigeria took London by storm.

    A. arrived in London by sea

    B. arrived in London during a storm

    C. were very popular with London spectators

    D. had very few spectators

482. Our discussion soon became animated.

    A. intellectual

    B. unruly

    C. lively

    D. robust

483. Bitrus' failure manifested when Bulus successfully worked up the mob.

   A. addressed

   B. implored

   C. incited

   D. indicted

484. The early bird catches the worm

   A. the person who arrives early will probably succeed

   B. the bird will catch the work early in the morning

   C. the worm will only be caught if it comes out early

   D. the person who catches the worm early will succeed.

485. The chairperson's anger was aggravated by the news of the disaster

   A. the disaster

   B. intensified

   C. magnified

   D. abated

   E. impeded

486. The arms dealer surreptitiously supplied arms to the two sides in the conflict.

   A. happily

   B. forcefully

   C. openly

   D. stealthily

487. The air in an industrial area is very often polluted.

    A.   hazy

    B.   filthy

    C.   dry

    D.   contaminated

in each of questions 488 to …. *choose the option opposite in meaning to the word(s) in italics.*

488. He mumble a few words at the trial and then fainted

    A.   cried

    B.   murmured

    C.   shouted

    D.   announced

489. Only people physically fit were selected

    A.   lazy

    B.   mature

    C.   unhealthy

    D.   agile

490. The principal's speech was very lively.

    A.   dull

    B.   short

    C.   emotional

    D.   sentimental

491. Abdullahi is a novice in tennis

    A. coach

    B. learner

    C. professional

    D. master

492. The mechanic is going to assemble my machine next week.

    A. dismantle

    B. repair

    C. dismember

    D. service

Use the words that best completes the gap.

493. The Minister has ordered……………….into the recent labour strike actions around the Country.

A.The probe B. a trial C . a probe D. the trial

494. She was arrested on -------------------- of robbery.

A. The grounding B. ground C. a ground D. The grounds.

495. Having failed in his first attempt, he wants to have……………..

  A. Re-trial B. a trial C.a try D. another try

496. Benjamin's mother instructed him to add……………..salt to the soup.

A. a few more B. a little more C .some few D. many more.

497. …………….rather remain broke than rob a bank and gun down innocent men and women.

A. I'd B .i'll C. would D. should

498. Bring that book……………mine.

A. It's B. he's C. it's D.it

499. ………………..the present circumstances , I think we have to retrace our steps.

A. with B. by C. in D.at

500. The quality of food in the boarding School has started to go ……………….. A. off B. out C. down D.back

FIVE HUNDRED (500) MODEL ANSWERS ON PAST GCSE A/LEVEL. EXAMINATIONS

1. E
2. B
3. D
4. A
5. E
6. C
7. A
8. B
9. C
10. E
11. E
12. B
13. A
14. D
15. D
16. A
17. A
18. A
19. B
20. C
21. A
22. A
23. E
24. A
25. B
26. C
27. D
28. D
29. C
30. A
31. C
32. A
33. D
34. B
35. B
36. C

#	Ans	#	Ans
37.	B	58.	B
38.	D	59.	A
39.	A	60.	D
40.	A	61.	D
41.	B	62.	D
42.	A	63.	A
43.	D	64.	C
44.	C	65.	B
45.	C	66.	C
46.	C	67.	E
47.	D	68.	B
48.	C	69.	B
49.	C	70.	E
50.	B	71.	A
51.	A	72.	A
52.	A	73.	C
53.	D	74.	E
54.	C	75.	A
55.	B	76.	A
56.	A	77.	E
57.	A	78.	E

79.	C	100.	C
80.	D	101.	B
81.	C	102.	E
82.	A	103.	B
83.	C	104.	A
84.	A	105.	D
85.	B	106.	D
86.	A	107.	E
87.	C	108.	D
88.	C	109.	B
89.	A	110.	C
90.	B	111.	A
91.	B	112.	E
92.	A	113.	A
93.	C	114.	C
94.	C	115.	A
95.	C	116.	A
96.	A	117.	A
97.	A	118.	A
98.	C	119.	B
99.	A	120.	A

121. A
122. A
123. A
124. A
125. D
126. B
127. B
128. B
129. A
130. C
131. C
132. B
133. E
134. A
135. D
136. A
137. B
138. C
139. B
140. D
141. B
142. C

143. C
144. C
145. C
146. D
147. B
148. D
149. B
150. B
151. D
152. D
153. E
154. C
155. A
156. E
157. A
158. D
159. B
160. D
161. A
162. B
163. C
164. E

165. E
166. B
167. C
168. D
169. D
170. D
171. A
172. C
173. B
174. C
175. A
176. C
177. B
178. B
179. B
180. C
181. B
182. A
183. A
184. B
185. C
186. A

187. C
188. C
189. A
190. A
191. D
192. B
193. A
194. B
195. A
196. D
197. C
198. B
199. B
200. A
201. A
202. C
203. D
204. C
205. E
206. B
207. D
208. D

209. B
210. C
211. E
212. D
213. B
214. B
215. C
216. B
217. E
218. E
219. C
220. C
221. B
222. E
223. B
224. B
225. B
226. D
227. C
228. A
229. D

230. D
231. A
232. B
233. E
234. A
235. B
236. B
237. C
238. C
239. A
240. D
241. D
242. C
243. D
244. C
245. C
246. C
247. B
248. C
249. D
250. C

251.	D	273.	D
252.	B	274.	A
253.	D	275.	D
254.	A	276.	C
255.	D	277.	D
256.	D	278.	A
257.	E	279.	A
258.	A	280.	C
259.	D	281.	A
260.	C	282.	A
261.	D	283.	C
262.	E	284.	C
263.	C	285.	C
264.	B	286.	B
265.	C	287.	B
266.	D	288.	C
267.	A	289.	C
268.	A	290.	D
269.	A	291.	A
270.	C	292.	C
271.	C	293.	C
272.	D	294.	A

295. B	317. B
296. D	318. B
297. C	319. A
298. A	320. B
299. A	321. B
300. B	322. A
301. C	323. D
302. A	324. D
303. C	325. C
304. C	326. B
305. C	327. B
306. B	328. C
307. B	329. B
308. A	330. A
309. C	331. B
310. C	332. A
311. D	333. A
312. A	334. A
313. A	335. C
314. C	336. C
315. B	337. D
316. D	338. A

339. A
340. B
341. B
342. B
343. B
344. B
345. B
346. D
347. B
348. C
349. D
350. D
351. A
352. B
353. C
354. B
355. D
356. B
357. C
358. B
359. B
360. B

361. C
362. A
363. C
364. A
365. C
366. A
367. A
368. C
369. A
370. A
371. C
372. A
373. D
374. C
375. D
376. B
377. B
378. C
379. A
380. B
381. C
382. C

383. A	406. B
384. D	407. C
385. A	408. B
386. A	409. A
387. C	410. A
388. C	411. C
389. A	412. D
390. C	413. B
391. C	414. A
392. B +C	415. A
393. A	416. A
394. B	417. D
395. B	418. D
396. C	419. D
397. A	420. B
398. C	421. C
399. A	422. C
400. C	423. B
401. B	424. C
402. C	425. D
403. B	426. A
404. C	427. A
405. A	428. B

429. C
430. C
431. B
432. A
433. C
434. B
435. C
436. C
437. D
438. A
439. D
440. B
441. D
442. B
443. D
444. B
445. A
446. C
447. B
448. D
449. A
450. D
451. C

452. B
453. A
454. C
455. B
456. A
457. C
458. D
459. D
460. A
461. B
462. A
463. D
464. A
465. B
466. A
467. D
468. B
469. B
470. D
471. B
472. A
473. A
474. B

475. C
476. D
477. C
478. B
479. B
480. A
481. C
482. C
483. C
484. A
485. B
486. D
487. D
488. C
489. C
490. A
491. C
492. A
493. C
494. D
495. A
496. A

497. A
498. A
499. C
500. C

www.ingramcontent.com/pod-product-compliance
Lightning Source LLC
Chambersburg PA
CBHW081351160426
43198CB00015B/2585